Nathan S. S. Beman

Thanksgiving in the Times of Civil War

Being a discourse delivered in the First Presbyterian church, Troy, New

York, Nov. 28th, 1861

Nathan S. S. Beman

Thanksgiving in the Times of Civil War
*Being a discourse delivered in the First Presbyterian church, Troy, New York, Nov.
28th, 1861*

ISBN/EAN: 9783337220891

Printed in Europe, USA, Canada, Australia, Japan

Cover: Foto ©Lupo / pixelio.de

More available books at **www.hansebooks.com**

THANKSGIVING

IN

THE TIMES OF CIVIL WAR:

BEING

𝔄 𝔇𝔦𝔰𝔠𝔬𝔲𝔯𝔰𝔢

DELIVERED IN THE

FIRST PRESBYTERIAN CHURCH,

TROY, NEW YORK,

NOV. 28TH, 1861.

BY N. S. S. BEMAN.

TROY, N. Y.:
A. W. SCRIBNER & CO., PRINTERS, CANNON PLACE.
1861.

TROY, November 30th, 1861.

N. S. S. BEMAN, D. D.,

Rev. and Dear Sir:

In view of the pleasure afforded by the delivery of your Sermon, of the 28th inst., upon "Thanksgiving in the Times of Civil War," we respectfully request a copy of it for publication, believing that its pure patriotism, and able vindication of the loyal North, will exert a wide and beneficent influence.

Very respectfully,

J. M. FRANCIS,
H. J. KING,
DAVID COWEE,
G. V. S. QUACKENBUSH,
M. I. TOWNSEND.

——— —— —— —— ——

TROY, December 2d, 1861.

To J. M. FRANCIS, H. J. KING, DAVID COWEE, G. V. S. QUACKENBUSH, AND M. I. TOWNSEND,

Gentlemen:

Your request is before me. The Discourse to which you refer, was prepared for the congregation to which I have long ministered, and I am gratified that it has been received with favor. In hopes, that its publication may still further promote the objects for which it was written, I cheerfully consign it to your disposal.

Very respectfully and truly yours,

N. S. S. BEMAN.

DISCOURSE.

"THE HEAVEN, EVEN THE HEAVENS, ARE THE LORD'S: BUT THE EARTH HATH HE GIVEN TO THE CHILDREN OF MEN."

THESE words are taken from a charming divine ode; and they form a gem in this finished oriental picture. And while this production is elevated in its subject-matter, and presented in the rich strains of Hebrew poetry, it is not inappropriate to this morning's convocation. The design, or purpose, of its author, is to inspire gratitude in the hearts of those for whom it was first written, and afterwards set to music, and then used in public worship. The mode in which he would compass this pious end, is a legitimate and natural one. He compares the condition of Israel with that of other nations, and especially in matters pertaining to theology, and the natural and necessary influence of different systems of belief on the moral and material interests of a people. Their correct notions of God, not less than the providence of God itself, had made them to differ from others.

The nations of the world, with all their high attainments—their philosophy and refinement—their progress in the arts of peace, and their skill and achievements in war, were blind idolaters. They had not formed the first conception of an infinite, personal, and spiritual God. Their deities were "dumb idols." They were not unfrequently material images in the form of men,—"silver and gold" and the like, and frequently of far baser materials. And while they were furnished with human organs, and were received and worshiped as gods, they exercised no powers of life or action. They were dumb, sightless, deaf,—and were devoid of the sense of smell and feeling. Their hands had no executive power, and their feet were incapable of locomotion. Such gods, and their makers and worshipers, formed a fit confraternity. "They that make them are like unto them; so is every one that trusteth in them."

But the Hebrews shared a happier lot. Of them it is written, "Ye are blessed of the Lord which made heaven and earth." The discriminating favors which lifted them far above the summit level of the heathen world, must not be buried in inglorious silence, but commemorated, by appropriate rites and observances. And these acts must be national, because a nation has an organic existence only in the present world. National devotion, and national retribution, are restricted to this life, while immortality cleaves only to the individual. "The Lord hath been mindful of us: he will bless us; he will bless the house of Israel; he will bless the house of Aaron. He will bless them that fear the Lord, both small and great. The Lord shall increase you more and more, you and your children. The heaven, even the heavens, are the Lord's: but the earth hath he given to the children of men. The dead"— whether nations or individuals—"praise not the Lord, neither they that go down into silence. But we"—the living, both in our associated and individual capacity—"will bless the Lord from this time forth and for ever-

more. Praise ye the Lord." This is strongly
national in its characteristics.

The main drift, or aim, of this inspired song,
is now before us. The text—"The heaven,
even the heavens, are the Lord's: but the earth
hath he given to the children of men,"—con-
tains a great thought, in keeping with the spirit
of the whole production, and will furnish the
suggestions for this occasion.

There are two declarations in the passage—
"The heaven, even the heavens, are the Lord's
—but the earth hath he given to the children
of men,"—and both of them must be taken
with certain needful restrictions. "The heaven,
even the heavens, are Jehovah's," not in the
sense, that it is the abode of his own solitary
and exclusive presence and grandeur, while
every other being is barred from its confines.
Angels are there. "The spirits of just men
made perfect," are there. In heaven is the
throne of God, and there is the home of his
glory. The law of God is the rule in that
world, and the will of God is done there,
universally, invariably, perfectly, and for ever.
It is not, like our world, the place for reclaim-
ing sinners, or of training imperfect moral

agents for eternal life. There is no government there but God's,—and no agency save his own divine efficiency, and that which sweetly accords with his gracious and benign will. In one word, God is all in all, there: and this justifies the declaration, that "The heaven, even the heavens, are the Lord's."

Heaven is God's best world, and the human eye is capable of catching a faint glimpse of its glories, as they are shined upon by the light of the scriptures. The pictures of heaven contained in the Bible, are, for the most part, combinations formed from elements selected from the attractive scenes and the brilliant objects of our world,—and these make their appeal both to our faith and imagination. A man of taste merely, must feel some interest in the gospel heaven, and a man of a pure heart and of lofty spiritual aspirations, cannot but wish to become a citizen of that kingdom where God is supreme, his will the sole law, and his glory the master-passion of every heart. That kingdom is heaven. "The heaven, even the heavens, are the Lord's." In this sense, that world is his. His throne stands there, and those who are like him, kneel down before it.

2

But the arrangements of God, and his disposals, are not confined to heaven. "The earth hath he given to the children of men." It was God's by creative power, and, by his own choice it became a gift to our race, in all coming generations. The ultimate end of all God's works, is, no doubt, his own glory. "Thou art worthy, O Lord, to receive glory, and honor and power: for thou hast created all things, and for thy pleasure they are and were created." But in creation, there are many subordinate ends, and in providence, there are long trains of connected causes and effects, all terminating in one ultimate end, and one final cause. God is that end, and that cause.

On this philosophical principle, we may say truly, that the *earth* was made for man, and given to him and his children. Look at the record of creation. The seven days employed in divine construction, by a regular gradation, culminated in man. He alone wore the divine image, and to him was given the diadem and dominion of the earth. This was his patrimony from the hand of God. "Be fruitful, and multiply, and replenish the earth, and subdue it." was the command of the munificent donor.

"The earth hath he given to the children of men."

This theory applies to the original creation. Before sin was conceived on earth, or Adam fell, this world was designed for man and his posterity. It was to be theirs through all generations. Not to the exclusion of God and his moral government. No. God could give the earth to men for their own use and purposes, and yet retain it for *his*. His ownership, or property, can be alienated in no part of his broad domains. By such an act, he would lay down 'his supremacy, and cease to be God. While, then, he has "given the earth to the children of men," he must for ever remain its physical and moral governor, and will be, its final judge; "for of him, and through him, and to him are all things,"

If man had remained loyal, and sin had never blighted our system, the earth would have presented a very different picture from that which now meets the eye. The precise state of things, must be a matter of conjecture, rather than certainty. I here see a green-clad and fruitful earth. Thorns and thistles there are none. Over head are brilliant heavens.

The air that is inhaled is balmy as the breath of
Spring: and no pestilence floats upon its bo-
som. But these, after all, are the mere append-
ages of a world,—the furniture and decorations
of the superb mansion. The higher perfection
must be looked for in man, the living inhabitant
of this magnificent building, the handy work
of the great architect. Fancy, then, to yourselves, what our earth, rich and gorgeous, and
fresh from the hand of its maker, must have
been without the stain of human sin upon it,—
one broad illimitable Eden—the primitive
walls removed, and Paradise made universal:
and all this glowing scene lighted up by one
brilliant luminary by day, and by a thousand
lesser, though chaster, diamond lamps by night,
—and you have a very natural conception of
a sinless world, as given to man and his posterity, at least in prospect, as "a goodly heritage."

And, then, if we ascend from the physical to
the intellectual and spiritual, what a race would
have peopled this globe! One that would
have appreciated the gift, and honored the
giver. Sin for ever barred access, it would
require but little imagination to teach us what
a world this must have been. The earth, in

accordance with the divine purpose, would
soon have been replenished and subdued,—
because no adverse elements would have ob-
structed the growth of population, or retarded
the progress of mind, or of productive skill, in
any thing great or good. What nations would
have covered, and cheered with intelligence
and enterprise, the continents and islands which
go to make up our globe! And not a dis-
cordant element among them all. There are
no wars—because no national encroachments
any where exist,—no thefts or robberies are
committed, because there is no avarice to
prompt to such deeds of villainy,—no assas-
sinations, because there is no malice to point
the steel, and nerve the arm, and deal the fatal
blow,—no disgraceful chains for the felon, for
crime there is none among men,—no slave
ship plows the wave, or slave mart, desecrates
the soil, for every one loves his neighbor as
himself, and cannot become an oppressor:—
and, in one word, in the repulsive forms in
which it now occurs—*no death!* Love to God
and love to man are the dominant affections
every where, while human governments are
easily administered, and salutary laws—and

all *are* such—well nigh execute themselves. The divine mechanism is perfect: and the moral machine with all its mysterious complications, moves in harmony.

But for the apostasy, this entire picture, more highly touched and finished, might have been seen in our world. The worship of the true God would have been universal, and "the higher law"—God's law—would have been the basis of all human legislation. The progress of man would have been restricted to no definable limits, and this world, in knowledge and goodness, would have been brought into near proximity to heaven. A thin partition wall only would have stood between them. Little more than a mathematical line, having length, but no breadth or thickness, would have separated and distinguished them from each other, and informed us where the one ended, and the other began.

But we must look at this gift of God to the children of men, in relation to the attitude of things as superinduced by the fall. This original grant was not annulled, or revoked, by the new moral position of our race. The earth is still their inheritance by divine charter. This is incidentally asserted by Paul in his address on Mars Hill, at Athens. He tells us, that God "hath made of one blood all nations of men, for to dwell on all the face of the earth, and hath determined the times before appointed, and the bounds of their habitation; that they should seek the Lord, if haply they might feel after him. and find him, though he be not far from every one of us."

Without attempting a critical analysis of this passage, I may say, that the following things are clearly taught, or fairly implied, in the language here used:—The unity of the human race;—they are "of one blood." God, in the beginning, created one human pair, and only one; and from these two sprang "all nations." The whole "face of the earth" was designed for "their habitation"—whether they should stand firm in their uprightness, or lapse into sin. This inheritance was to be free and open to all; and all might seek and secure, as responsible moral agents, the great objects of human life. Nor was this charter vacated. by the fall. This fact is assumed by the Apostle. The same rule was to obtain, and the same rights to be enjoyed, under the gospel as a remedial system, as under the primitive law. Indeed, he applies the principle especially to the present existing state of the world and its nations. He made them, and ordered their lot, as he has, " That they should seek the Lord, if haply they might feel after him, and find him."

There are certain great principles, not less of morals and religion, than of politics and jurisprudence, set forth in the " DECLARATION OF INDEPENDENCE," which are now characterized, in certain quarters, for special purposes, as " rhetorical flourishes," and "glittering generalities," that might find their prototype in this charter of human rights drawn up by Paul, and announced in the celebrated Areopagus. If we could trace intuitively the subtle processes of thought, and follow its electric flash from one master-mind to another, we might feel ourselves not less indebted to the apostle Paul than to Thomas Jefferson, for such foundation principles as these: " We hold these truths to be self-evident—that all men are created equal; that they are endowed by their Creator with certain unalienable rights; that among these are life, liberty, and the pursuit of happiness. That to secure these rights, gov-

peopling of the earth, according to the purpose of God, presents a fruitful subject of research, as a matter of history,—and the origin, growth, and subversion of empires, are not less so, as matters of profound philosophy. But these cannot be disposed of in a single sermon. Both of them—only as they occur incidentally—must be passed in silence.

That God intended men to occupy his gift, by settling the earth and cultivating it, may be learned not only from the fact, that he uttered a command to this effect, but when they were slow to obey this command, and seemed determined to cluster around their birth-place and their cradle, and live and die there, he wrought a special miracle for their dispersion. This miracle was the origin of nations. How far the physical elements of different countries contributed to form and perpetuate national characteristics, I must not inquire now. Their influence was, no doubt, great, if not paramount; but I have other things in view to-day.

The gift of the earth to " the children of

3

men," was a munificent one, and a benevolence not second to the gift itself, characterized the donation. I speak of the earth now, as prospectively a fallen sphere—where adverse passions would meet in sad conflict, and where dependent moral agents, under the government of God, must solve the great problems of life, and work out an immortal destiny. Look at the charter again. "The earth hath he given to the children of men." And in other and new circumstances too, adapted to the present state of things, as cited by Paul: "And hath made of one blood all nations of men for to dwell on all the face of the earth."

Peace and not war, on these principles, should have been the normal state of man; and the arts of peace, and not the tactics and achievements of war, should have called forth his best powers, and constituted his great life-work. How far this has been the case, may be judged of by such facts as these. Human history is little else than a record of sieges and battles. Take a few specimens touching the destruction of life by this one agency.

"Do you ask, then, for an epitome of the havoc war has made of human life? In the

Russian campaign there perished in less than six months nearly half a million of French alone, and perhaps as many more of their enemies. Napoleon's wars sacrificed full six millions, and all the wars consequent on the French Revolution, some nine or ten millions. The Spaniards are said to have destroyed in forty-two years more than twelve millions of American Indians. The wars in the time of Sesostris cost 15.000.000 lives; those of Semiramis, Cyrus, and Alexander, ten millions each; those of Alexander's successors, 20.000.000. Grecian wars sacrificed 15.000.000 ; Jewish wars, 25.000.000; the wars of the twelve Cæsars, 30.000.000 in all; the wars of the Roman empire, of the Saracens, and the Turks, 60.000.000 each; the wars of the Reformation, 30.000.000; those of the Middle Ages, and the nine Crusades in two centuries, 40.000.000 each; those of the Tartars, 80.000.000 ; those of Africa 100.000.000 ! If we take into consideration," says the learned Dr. Dick, "the number, not only of those who have fallen in battle, but of those who perished by the natural consequences of war, it will not perhaps be overrating the destruction of human life, if we affirm, that *one-tenth* of the human race has been destroyed by the ravages of war; and, according to this estimate, more than *fourteen thousand millions* of human beings have been slaughtered in war since the beginning of the world." Edmund Burke went still further, and reckoned the sum total of its ravages from the first, at no less than *thirty-five thousand millions ! ! ***

These few facts, selected from many of the like character, show that war has been the great business of our wretched world.

The primitive dispersion of our race, not only peopled the earth, but each separate tribe, or distinct family, formed the basis of a national organization. This fact may be distinctly traced by the lights of ancient history. And not only so, but this arrangement was vital to the interests of human progress. The expanding race could no more form one vast nation, and live, to advantage, under one consolidated dynasty, than a great city, like London or Paris, could be included in the same family circle, and live happily and profitably under one sheltering roof. Human government *now*

* See Beckwith's Peace Manual, p. p. 11, 42.

for the first time, becomes a necessity. Before this event, little more existed, or was needed, than the unwritten law of the patriarch of the home circle. And it is not at all strange, that there should be some diversity, in the primitive form and administration of government,—commencing with the more absolute, because the more simple, and becoming more liberal and popular, as men became more intelligent and active. Civil government was ordained of God,—but the type and form were not.— These are incidentals, and not essentials, of the system. They are among the prerogatives secured to beings who wear their Maker's image, by the ordinance of heaven. Government there should be, and *must* be, or God is both disobeyed, and dishonored,—but the form is left to the option and agency of man. And notwithstanding the storms which are beating upon the frame-work of our Republic, at this day, and subjecting the solidity of the basis and the strength of the superstructure to a severe test—I stand where I ever have stood, the declared and unwavering advocate of a free, elective government. But this position may need some explanations before I close.

Any citizen has a right to demand a defence, or an apology.

In glancing the eye over the map of nations, and estimating their position and advantages, and their material resources, we find special cause for gratitude to the sovereign disposer for his munificence to us, as a people. It is not necessary to affirm, that we possess every thing, and other nations, nothing. This is a vain boast of which we have had too much. It is unseemly before men, and offensive to heaven. But if we look at all the elements which go to make up the glory of a country, what other national inheritance can compare with ours? Think of its broad and extended area, the fertility of its soil, the variety of its products, the salubrity of its climate, and the picturesque beauty and grandeur of its scenery, —lakes, prairies, rivers, forests, mountains: and all these, too, on a scale to be found no where else—gigantic in their magnificence—delight-fully combined and intermingled in the picture —displaying light and shade, and presenting an outline, a filling up, and a coloring, no where else to be seen on the surface of this great globe.

Nor are these physical elements our chief
distinctions. This fair field was planted with
the best seed-corn of Europe—carefully selected and well winnowed, before it was dropped
into the virgin soil. And, then, the harvest
which it has for the most part spread out in
the sun-light of heaven, has been truly cheering. During most of our history, war has
disturbed us but little, while industry and the
arts of peace, have wrought changes in the
United States which may challenge a terres-
trial parallel. I need not tell you of the
primeval forests which have been felled, and
the broad acres which have been laid open to
the sun, and been subjected to the plow-share,
yielding a rich return,—how villages have
studded the valleys, and farm-houses starred
the mountain sides, and cities sprung up, like
magic, along the coast, and on the margin of
the great rivers,—nor how our merchant ves-
sels have whitened and beautified every sea,—
and, on their return, poured the wealth of
nations into our lap. A hint is enough, and
the activities of *memory* are stirred up, and all
is before you. And our commonwealth, especially, has shared, without stint, in these smiles

of heaven, on our land. This Autumnal Festival, is a fit occasion for our thankoffering as a people. " Praise ye the Lord."

But here a grave question presents itself, in connection with the existing attitude of our country. We are involved in a civil war—the worst of all wars of course,—and there are men so intensely absorbed by one idea, that they doubt whether we are called upon to lift up the joyous note of thanksgiving for any thing we have left. This is a narrow view of a broad subject. A sad picture, it is true, meets the eye, but all is not lost. We have a government yet, and I trust in heaven, that government will stand. It is not at all strange, that the crowned heads and starred shoulders of the old world, should turn a leering look upon us in the day of our adversity. They have never forgiven us for the rash act of achieving our own independence. They have been looking, for half a century, for our downfall,—and many of them have died without the sight. I hope many more may follow in their inglorious wake. It requires, however, a little more than an ordinary stock of self-possession to bear with England in some of her false positions, at the present day. No one can fail to see the hard struggle that is going on between pelf and principle—between her conscience and her circumstances; so that, if she were to enter upon a personal vindication, it might be expressed on this wise,—'Not that we love freedom and the North less. but cotton and the other products of slave-labor, more.'

But however humiliating our condition, and however severe and decisive the crisis may prove itself to be, we are not to infer, as some among ourselves, and many across the waters, have done, that we are a ruined nation, and the government is annihilated, because we are involved in a civil war. What country in Europe—I might almost say, the *world*—has not been lashed by the same tempest,—and some of them, again and again! England, France, Germany, Spain, Portugal, Italy— have all been swept and desolated by this bloody scourge, and yet their governments have withstood the shock, or been exchanged for better ones; and the nations—or many of them, have not only survived, but prospered. A single civil war in England lasted thirty years; and this was only one of many. And

4

the whole matter at stake, in this long, deadly
strife, was the right of succession to the throne!
A few pages of Anglican history. well conned,
might greatly modify certain articles in the
London Times, and correct many strange positions and croaking prophecies of their self-
satisfied and arrogant correspondent—the *fast
rider*—Dr. Russell, now hanging about Wash-
ington City. But as I am for toleration, and
the largest liberty, I would not drive him
away, *but let him hang there.*

A great poet and an acute thinker, has said,
"There are many things between the heavens
and the earth, which our philosophy dreameth
not of." But living two and a half centuries
later than the author, we might say, 'There are
many things on the earth, without going one
inch towards heaven—which neither our philosophy, nor imagination, could dream of before
they were embodied in facts before us.' Who,
when the Constitution of the United States was
formed, or fifty years ago, in his most feverish
and delirious dreams, could have believed, or
even fancied. that any portion of our common
country would have waged war against another,
—and especially for the causes alledged?

What are the complaints of the South against
the government? Have they been oppressed,
so that further endurance has become insup-
portable? Let us look at the case, and see if
the charge is true. Some northern men say it
is: and if we can believe the South, they have
been forced to take the step of secession first,
and then the attitude of armed resistance to
the government, from the same sacred motives
which impelled our patriot fathers to break off
their allegiance to the mother country. Ex-
amine the two cases, and see if the pretended
analogy does not turn out a downright *contrast*
rather. Had the Colonies any control over
the executive, the British King? None at all,
either in setting him on the throne, or ordering
him down. And yet the South with her
meager population has given us eight presi-
dents, and the North with an excess of millions,
only seven when this southern revolt was fully
inaugurated. Had the Colonies any voice in
the Legislature, the English parliament? Not
any. Yet the very slaves of the South have
placed on the floor of Congress, from twenty
to twenty-five members, as a bonus, or as a
gratuity, for their peculiar institution. Had

we any thing to do with the Judiciary of
England? Nothing, except to stand as felons,
after a long sea voyage, before their courts,
and receive sentence,—while the South have,
most of the time since we have been a government, controlled the national Bench; and,
for the last sixty years, the presiding officer,
the Chief Justice, has been a southern man
and a slaveholder. Have any petitions for
the removal of grievances been disregarded?
None: for no such have been offered. The
South have generally controlled the government,—and to present a memorial against
grievances, or a petition for special favors,
would be an act of supererogation, or of mock
humility: as much so as it would have been
in "the elder son," in the Parable, to ask the
father for "a kid," that he "might make merry
with his friends,"—and the reply would have
been the same. "Son, thou art ever with me;
and all that I have is thine."

As to the Constitution itself, it is strongly
southern in several of its provisions, as every
one knows, who has studied it with care. The
spirit of slave encroachment had begun to
work before this instrument was formed. But

let this pass, as it does not concern us now.
It is alledged, that the Constitution has be n
violated to the injury and oppression of the
South; and this charge has sometimes been
uttered by northern lips. But is it so? I
have failed to discover such a fact. The great
matters of complaint, gleaned from acres of
controversy, may be summed up in the following things. There are only three. The sentiments of the North, on the subject of chattel
slavery, are utterly unsound and heretical.
So the South alledge. We hold that the whole
system is contrary to the law of God and
nature, and opposed to the moral sense of man,
—and that, in its practical results, it is a great
political and moral evil,—inflicting about equal
calamities on masters and slaves, and cursing
the very soil that bears it. And we claim the
right to speak out our sentiments, on this as on
all other great questions, in the pulpit, on the
platform, and every where among freemen.
Is this unconstitutional? It has always been
done—when the Constitution was formed, and
ever since.

But there is a worse political heresy than
this held at the North, and by a majority of

the American people,—That slavery is a local institution, and is subject only to municipal laws, and must of course be confined to those states which are subject to a slave code. It cannot travel abroad and carry these local statutes with it, and thus render them general, or universal. Hence the TERRITORIES are barred against this institution, till some power having the control of them, shall form a local slave code for their government. Is there any thing unconstitutional in all this? Is not this leaving the matter just where the Constitution has placed it? You can all judge, and all speak, for yourselves.

But a graver charge than all, remains to be named. Fugitives from service—or fugitive slaves, have not been returned, in good faith, according to the provisions of the Constitution. Two or three things should be looked at, in connection with this charge. The GOVERNMENT has not refused to regard this law. Two or three administrations have made it a leading object of their high vocation to chase every man with a dark skin whose face was turned toward the herald star of freedom—the North Pole,—and to return him to hopeless bondage.

And, then, some of the provisions of the existing fugitive slave law are such, that no one but a genuine Shylock could wish to see it executed. One whose hand was prominent in its construction, is reported to have said, that he aimed to make it so odious that it never would be executed. The motive can be no mystery. That gentleman is now in Fort Warren. More than all this, the State that took the lead in this rebellion, and those that soon followed this bad example, had suffered less than many others from this cause. They had rarely lost a slave. And, then, I have noticed another fact worthy of record. In the few cases of rescue which have taken place, here and there, the popular sympathies have generally flowed in one direction,—so that some of the strongest pro-slavery advocates have been the loudest in crying *amen*, when the hunted victim, panting for freedom, had made good his escape. It was *nature's* utterance, without waiting to theorize. Some would say, the voice of God speaking in man.

So much for alledged violations of the Constitution. We may now glance at the novel constructions put upon this instrument by

southern politicians—I cannot call them states-
men. In politics, as in philosophy, men often
fin', or think they do, what they are looking
for. The leading secessionists can see in the
constitutional provision for the return of their
fugitive chattels, and a few other incidental
recognitions of slavery, that this institution is
the prime element of our system, and that it
pervades everything, and can go every where,
without asking leave, and that it is a crime,
deserving "strangling and death," to breathe a
doubt whether it is heaven-born and heaven-
descended! It may go to Kansas, plant itself
in New Mexico, or Nebraska, and repose luxu-
riously under the shadow of the Bunker Hill
monument,—and no lover of the Constitution
should lift a voice or finger against it. If any
man should chance to feel some scruples
against such license,—'*for peace sake, let him
keep silent!*' One of the great men of the
South, now paying court to the pioneer anti-
slavery Kingdom of Europe, and receiving
marked attentions there it is said, has discov-
ered, that the prohibition of the African slave
trade was unconstitutional,—when that instrument had made a special provision, that such

an act might be passed, as early as 1808.
The South may be set down as *progressive*:—
for they discover new things in the Constitution, just as fast as they are needed. Once
they held as everybody else did, that it tolerated slavery in the States, merely as a state
institution, and gave certain limited and well
defined privileges for the security of these state
rights. But now, though they are all strict
constructionists, they can see in these facts of
toleration, or sufferance, few and well guarded
as they are, that slavery is the life-blood and
animating spirit of the whole system, that it is
the corner stone of the Republic, that there
can be no rational liberty without it, and that
our government was framed to defend, enlarge,
and perpetuate human bondage, rather than
freedom. In one word, they find in the Constitution, just what they are seeking for.

"The passions," says Helvetius, as cited by
Sir Wm. Hamilton, in his Lectures on Philosophy, "not only concentrate our attention on
certain exclusive aspects of the object which
they present, but they likewise often deceive
us in showing those same objects where they
do not exist. The story is well known of a
5

parson and a gay lady. They had both heard that the moon was peopled, — *believed it*, — and, telescope in hand, were attempting to discover the inhabitants. If I am not mistaken, says the lady, who looked first, I perceive two shadows; they bend towards each other, and I have no doubt, are two happy lovers. Lovers, madame, says the divine, who looked second; oh fie! the two shadows you saw are the two steeples of a cathedral. The story is the history of man. In general, we perceive only in things what we are desirous of finding: on the earth as in the moon, various prepossessions make us always recognize either lovers or cathedrals." On this principle, the South see all they wish to see in the Constitution. They believe it all before they look into the telescope; and then submit to scrutiny the objects of their research.

I have adverted to the reasons which have been assigned in justification of this rebellion. They are in the main too shallow to impose upon the most credulous; and I shall not argue the case, for every one knows, that the grand motive is to glorify slavery. But this strange enterprise — the strangest that ever

astonished the world, like a clap of thunder
from a clear sky—is as inexpedient, as it is
causeless, on the part of its projectors. To
say nothing of the bad spirit the South has
long cherished towards the North, the bitter
denunciations which have characterized long
years of controversy, and the crowning act of
all, in opening the floodgates of death upon us
—thus hazarding the reprobation of the civilized world against themselves:—their better
genius must have forsaken them, and stood
aloof from their councils, when they staked all
on this deadly strife with the government.
The world is instinctively against rebellion,
unless "the powers that be" are known to be
oppressive. And they must be notoriously so.
The fact must not admit of a shadow of a
doubt. And can this be affirmed of our government? There is not a corner of the world,
where the lightness of our burdens, our just
and equal laws, our security of person and
property—so far as white men are concerned,
are not celebrated in notes that make the earth
resound, and reach heaven. And, then, their
position as to slavery and the slave trade, is
such as to entitle them to no sympathy from

abroad, and if it had not been for the single fact that Europe wants cotton — *must have* cotton — the universal christian and civilized world would have united in heaping curses on the heads of these insurgents against the mildest government on earth, ponderous enough " to sink a navy."

And, then, as to their own material interests, could infatuation ever exceed theirs! They are fast exhausting all their home supplies, and their intercourse with the North, and with foreign countries, is well nigh cut off, while their only products which bring a return in money, lie a dead weight upon their hands. A strong fortification of our own military posts and a strict enforcement of the blockade, would have parallized, in two years, every available energy of soul, and body, and purse, without expending an ounce of powder or a pound of lead. I do not say this course should have been pursued, but I would merely indicate the perils of their position. The winter that is now setting in, will pinch rebellion *black and blue*, and it would do it more effectually, if there were no men among us, who have stronger sympathies with traitors, than with

their good old mother, who has ever "nour-
isl.ed and brought" them up as "children."

There is a certain class of persons, or things
—for the Constitution seems to contemplate
them in the one light, and the State laws in the
other—but who are now very happily termed
CONTRABANDS,—who bear a very important
relation to the existing civil war. Their labor
will become less and less valuable to their
owners, as this strife waxes hotter and hotter.
The planting interests of portions of Virginia,
are desolated already by their perverse notions
of liberty; and this phrensy will travel on as
our majestic and cherished Eagle shall face the
sun, and look him straight in the eye. There
are men among us—and good men, too, I
have no doubt, who beg us not to mix up the
slave question with this war. If this is intended merely to enter a protest, that we are
not carrying on this strife for the *abolition* of
slavery, I cheerfully subscribe it. Nor are we
fighting for the *defence* of slavery. This would
be infinitely foolish. The traitors are doing
this; and if we join them in the object, both
armies should be one.

But slavery, in spite of *our* acts, will mingle

itself with this war, and no power on earth can prevent it. If chattels abscond from their owners, are our armies to chase and capture them, and carry them home again? This would be very polite. If they come to us, shall we send them back to aid the rebels, or set them to work, that they may aid us? And, moreover, if neither we nor the slaves mix up this war with the peculiar institution, their masters will do it. They *have* done it. They are doing it every day. They employ their slaves in erecting fortifications, in the transportion of military stores, as teamsters on the highway, in hard labor and menial services of every kind, and especially in *cooking*,—and in the last mentioned office, a *slave* is as indispensable as *eating*. Among the real chivalry, the latter must cease when the former is gone. And the time may come when this class will be compelled to fight for their owners. You might as well return horses, or breadstuffs, or fire-arms, to the enemy as slaves. And when this war shall rage with a firmness and desperation which may be before us, we shall learn philosophy from an old poet, that

" You take my house, when you do take the prop
That doth sustain my house."

Slavery is the prop that sustains the Southern Confederacy,—it could not stand a day without it. And as the war power, and especially that of a civil war, has the supreme control in this matter, the time is probably at hand, when the cotton rebellion and slavery will fall together. If this rebellion is not quelled soon, slavery is sure to go down with it.

But it may be asked, shall we liberate the slaves, and arm them to cut the throats of their masters? By no means. It is not implied in anything I have suggested. The African race are mild and pacific to a proverb; and there is but one thing for which they would unite in promiscuous assassination, and that is *liberty*. Give them this boon, and they would love their masters, and leave them too, and let them alone. Patrick Henry, for aught I know, was inspired with that burst of eloquence—"Give me liberty, or give me death"—by having seen slavery as it is. Some old Virginia bondman, gray-headed, and crushed in spirit, and soul, and body, sat for that picture, which, in his eye, seemed worse than death itself. And in the stern and grim face of this civil war, I see one benign feature. When the records of

this world shall be spread out in the light of
another, we may learn that this very national
calamity under which we all groan, was the
very event under a gracious, overruling providence, which forestalled and prevented another
St. Domingo massacre on this continent. God
seems at this day to have taken the cause of
the slave into his own keeping, and we may
be content with stating our principles, and
leave the rest with Him. My own opinion is,
and I impose it on nobody else, that this war
and the institution of slavery in North America, will end together. It expired thus in
portions of South America, and I should be
sorry to think that we are less enlightened, less
humane, or less the friends of liberty, than
they. On the mode of closing up this matter,
I have no theory to broach. But this much I
wish to say. To loyal men I would have the
government make a fair compensation for their
losses: for they were "faithful found among
the faithless." To the rebels, I would allow
nothing. Their claim is barred by the Constitution. They have put themselves out of the
Union, and the government is bound by no
compact to return their fugitives. And they

are the last men on earth to whom such an act should be accorded on the ground of comity. Some other things would much better comport with their position and character. Whether they will have those other things — is not for me to say.

There are some even in the loyal states, who are disposed to carry a white flag, and affect soft language, and practice genuflections, as they approach rebels armed to the teeth, and breathing out slaughter and death against the government and every man at the North. Thank heaven, there are not many such among us. They are "few, and far between." They look like grasshoppers after a hard autumnal frost, or a sweeping equinoctial storm, lone and pensive, carrying on their secret communings with one another only by suppressed and mysterious whispers. Every victory for their own dear native soil and freedom, is followed by a deep groan over this fatricidal war; and the only lifting up of the dark cloud from their brow, and the only glimmerings of hope which play around their features and spread a broad sunshine over all the face, is when such events as the fall of Sumter, or the disaster of Big

6

Bethel, the flight of Bull Run, or the slaughter of Ball's Bluff, are heralded in the newspapers. Every keen eye has seen all this, and taken note of it. Such things are not to be forgotten. They may be of use at some future day,—it may be of retribution—certainly of historical reminiscence.

There are a few things which ought to be definitely settled by all loyal citizens. The times demand both wisdom and honesty. It is too late now to attempt to deceive ourselves, or to impose upon others. The nation is engaged in a bloody strife, traitors have assailed the government, and life or death hangs on the issue. There can be no neutrality. Every man's influence, action, *prayers*—if he pray at all—must contribute moral or material power to the government, or to its sworn enemies. Let every one take his position—take sides— for there is not an inch of neutral ground to stand upon. And the greater the decision, the shorter the conflict. If any sympathize with the South—which some very poorly conceal —let them go down to the land they love, and partake of "the milk and honey" of a slave *regime*, and share its fate. If it were in my

heart to wish them *penance* and *purgation*, I
would not say more. Such persons do not
belong here. This soil and climate do not suit
them. There is some mistake in their birth
place and home.

But in making your choice, and giving
shape to your future energies, please to take
note of the following things. Slavery lies at
the basis of this insurrection,—not slavery as
it is tolerated and protected by the Constitution—but *slave propagandism*, which is not to
be satisfied till the whole land and all its institutions reflect its dark hues, and are put under
its feet. The right of secession is an absurdity,
in political compacts; and coersion is conse-
quently the duty of every government which
is not willing to yield its assent to self-annihi-
lation. The insurrectionists having attacked
the government and its loyal supporters, resistance is imperative, if we would not abandon
self-respect, and incur the scorn and derision
of the world.

This is our position, and there is no escape
from it. Talk of compromise with traitors!
Propose concessions under the dictation of the
slave lash! And what concessions? Why,

such as would yield more than two-thirds of all our territory and most of the grand outlets of commerce to the ocean, into the hands of the insurgents. To say nothing of the burning shame of such an act — what material good would be left to us? A mere skeleton of a Republic, which just now promised to be second to no power on earth. Besides all this, what a neighbor should we have! One ever stimulated by inextinguishable hate, prosecuting constant inroads, and meditating further dismemberments of our domain. The men are stark mad, who talk of *compromise*.

There are some things that are not to be admitted, — the very thought cannot be entertained. And the things I have named are among them. No, never! Better that a whole generation of the American people perish in this fearful struggle of order against misrule, than that our government and all the high expectations of freedom and progress which have been inspired by our institutions throughout the world, be blotted out in this one sad drama, and its bloody catastrophe. May heaven forbid, — may God, in mercy and sovereignty, forestall such a doom.

There is but one course left for us. We have no choice in the matter, if we do our duty and bide our lot. We must stand around the Ark of our civil and political Covenant, and never surrender it into the hands of the Philistines. God gave it to us, and we must defend it, come life, if it may,—come death, if it must. Let the North present one unbroken front to the disloyal and faithless foe—with not a traitor in the camp. Such a personage should be welcomed no where—should be tolerated no where, except at Fort Warren.

" In the name of our God we will set up our banners." This is no common warfare. We have not entered upon it for conquest—or fame—or to gratify some old revenge ; but are forced into it, for the protection of civil government—"the ordinance of God." This work is committed to our hands, and we dare not betray our hearts. Self-preservation, too, spurs us on to the conflict. The Union must be preserved,—treason, if God permit, shall be rebuked. Let our armies go forth then, to the battle with brave hearts, and strong hands, and fearless steps, in the name of God and freedom, and my faith shall wait quietly for the result,

—while the old Flag of the nation is given to the breeze. It it the "STAR SPANGLED BANNER," fragrant with cherished memories,—rich in cheering anticipations. Let this banner float—while the free winds of heaven shake out its gorgeous folds, and the sun shine upon its stars and stripes, till a mellow light shall cover this whole scene of grandeur and glory.

"Then conquer we must, when our cause it is just,
And this be our motto—"IN GOD IS OUR TRUST!"
And the star spangled banner in triumph shall wave,
O'er the land of the free, and the home of the brave."

www.ingramcontent.com/pod-product-compliance
Lightning Source LLC
Chambersburg PA
CBHW021435090426
42739CB00009B/1492